How to Write Hiragana and Katakana

The strokes of hiragana and katakana are always written from left to right and from top to bottom. Each stroke will have one of the following types of ending: とめ **tome** (stop), はね **hane** (jump) or はらい **harai** (sweep). A stop is when the stroke comes to a stop before you move your pen from the paper. A jump is a small flourish made by removing the pen from the paper as you move to the next stroke. A sweep is when the pen is slowly removed from the end of the stroke in a sweeping motion. In the letter **ke** shown on the right, stroke 1 is a jump, stroke 2 is a stop and stroke 3 is a sweep.

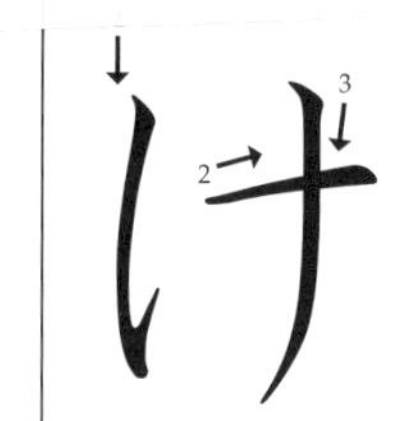

Stroke Orders for Writing Hiragana Characters

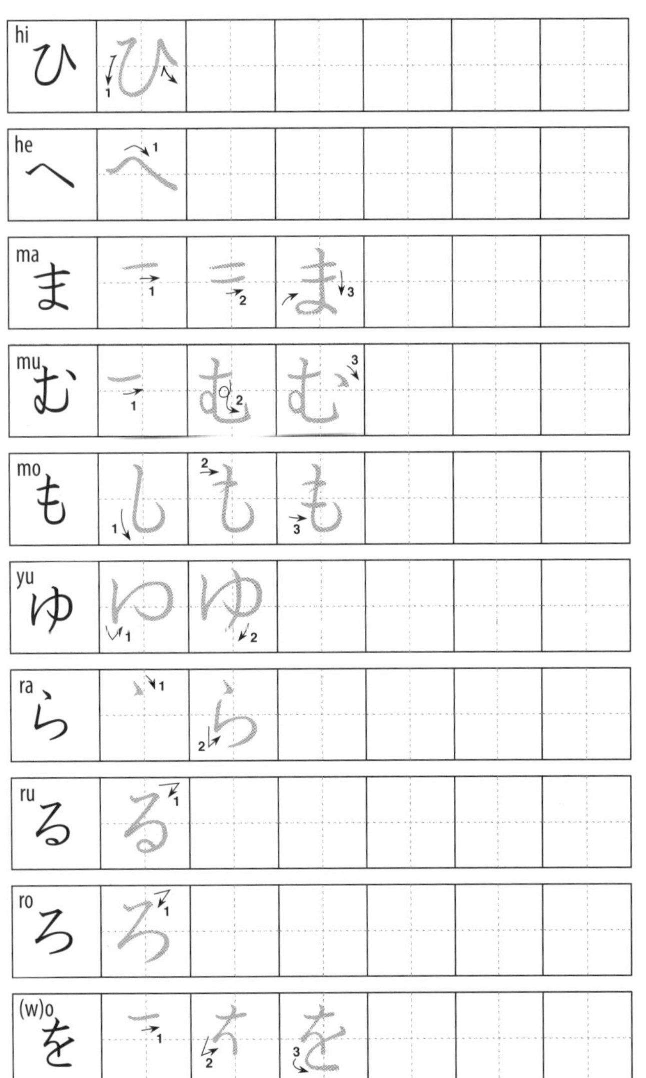

Stroke Orders for Writing Katakana Characters

su	ス
so	ソ
chi	チ
te	テ
na	ナ
nu	ヌ
no	ノ
hi	ヒ
he	ヘ
ma	マ
mu	ム
mo	モ
yu	ユ
ra	ラ
ru	ル
ro	ロ
(w)o	ヲ

se	セ
ta	タ
tsu	ツ
to	ト
ni	ニ
ne	ネ
ha	ハ
fu	フ
ho	ホ
mi	ミ
me	メ
ya	ヤ
yo	ヨ
ri	リ
re	レ
wa	ワ
n	ン

How to Write Kanji Characters

To write kanji properly and legibly, it is very important to know how each stroke is drawn. Here are some principles and tendencies for stroke endings, stroke directions and stroke orders.

Stroke Endings

Each stroke ends in とめ **tome** (stop), はね **hane** (jump) or はらい **harai** (sweep). (Note that some diagonal lines end in stop-sweep.) For example, a vertical straight line can end in stop, jump, or sweep, as shown below:

Stroke Directions

A stroke can be vertical, horizontal, diagonal, angled, or curved, or can be just a short abbreviated line.

Vertical lines always go from top to bottom, and *horizontal lines* always go from left to right.

Diagonal lines can go either downward or upward. For example:

If a stroke forms a corner, a sharp angle, or a curve, it goes from left to right and then goes down, or goes down and then left to right. For example:

corner

sharp angle

curve

Some strokes have a combination of a sharp angle and a curve. For example:

Some strokes are extremely short and are called てん **ten**. They may be vertical or slightly diagonal:

Stroke Order

You should remember how the strokes in each character are ordered in order to write a character neatly with the appropriate shape. Most kanji characters are written following the general principles of stroke order:

1. From top to bottom.

三 (three)

2. From left to right.

川 (river)

3. Horizontal strokes usually precede vertical strokes when crossing, although there are some exceptions such as 王 and 田.

十 (ten)

4. A central line usually precedes the strokes placed on its right and left.

小 (small)

5. An outer frame must be written first before finishing the inside except for the bottom line. The bottom line of an outer frame must be completed at the very end.

国 (country)

6. A right-to-left diagonal stroke precedes a left-to-right diagonal stroke.

人 (person)

7. A vertical line piercing through the center of a character is written last.

車 (vehicle)

8. A horizontal line piercing the center of the character is written last.

子 (child)

How to Write 32 Basic Kanji Characters

四	shi/yo-	**four**
五	go/itsu-	**five**
六	roku/mu-	**six**
七	shichi/nana-	**seven**
百	hyaku	**100**
千	sen/chi	**1,000**
万	man/ban	**10,000**
円	en/maru-	**yen/circle**

日
nichi/hi
sun/day

月
tsuki/gatsu
moon/month

火
hi/ka
fire

水
sui/mizu
water

木
moku/ki
wood/tree

金
kin/kane
gold

土
do/tsuchi
earth

週
shū
week

年
nen/toshi
year

時
ji/toki
time

間
kan/aida
between

分
bun/wa-
minute

午
go/uma
noon

前
zen/mae
before

後
go/ushi
after

今
kon/ima
now

半 han/naka **half**	1	2	3	4	5	半	半	半			
何 ka/nani **what**	1	2	3	4	5	6	7	何	何	何	
川 sen/kawa **river**	1	2	3	川	川	川					
山 san/yama **mountain**	1	2	3	山	山	山					
女 jo/onna **woman**	1	2	3	女	女	女					
男 dan/otoko **man**	1	2	3	4	5	6	7	男	男	男	
子 shi/ko **child**	1	2	3	子	子	子					
友 to yū/tomo **friend**	1	2	3	4	友	友	友				

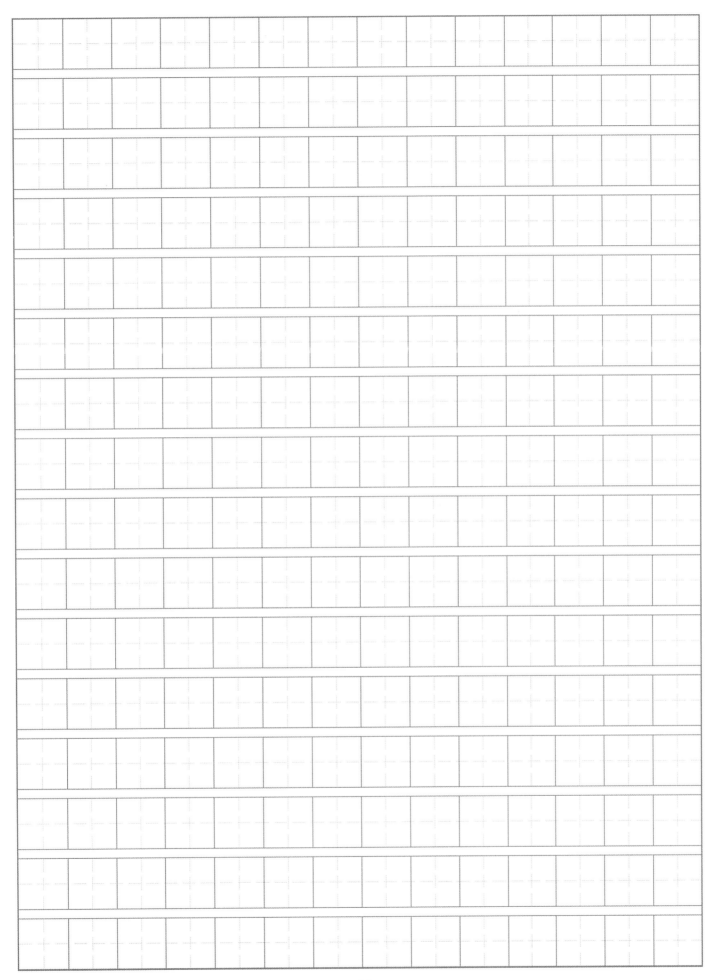

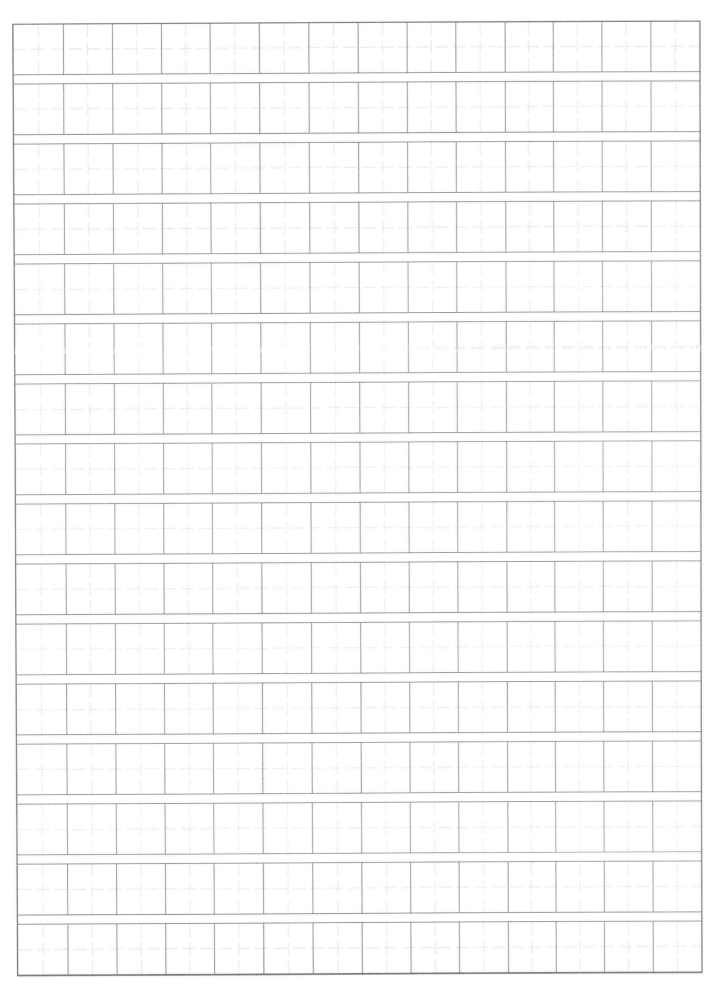

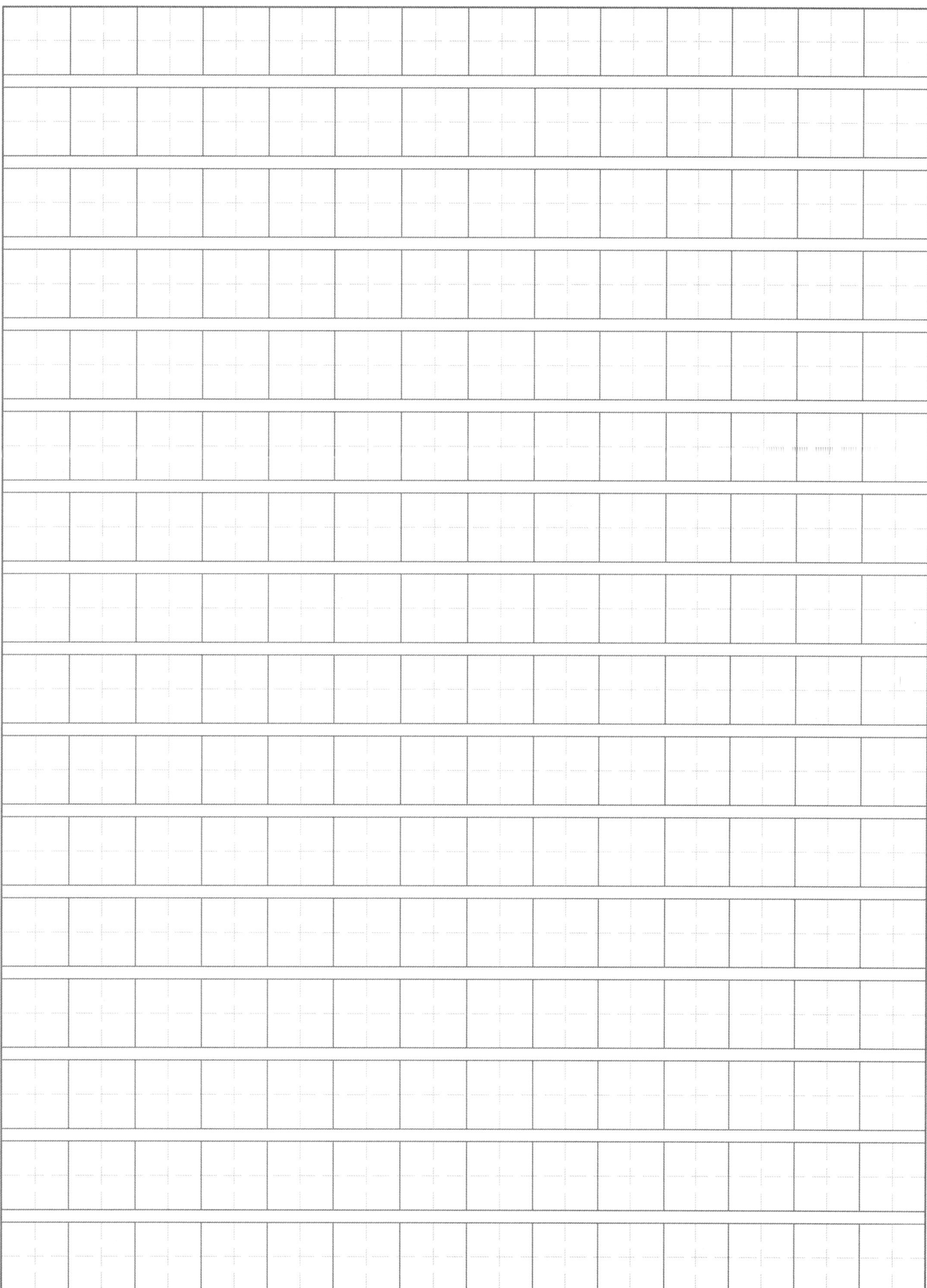

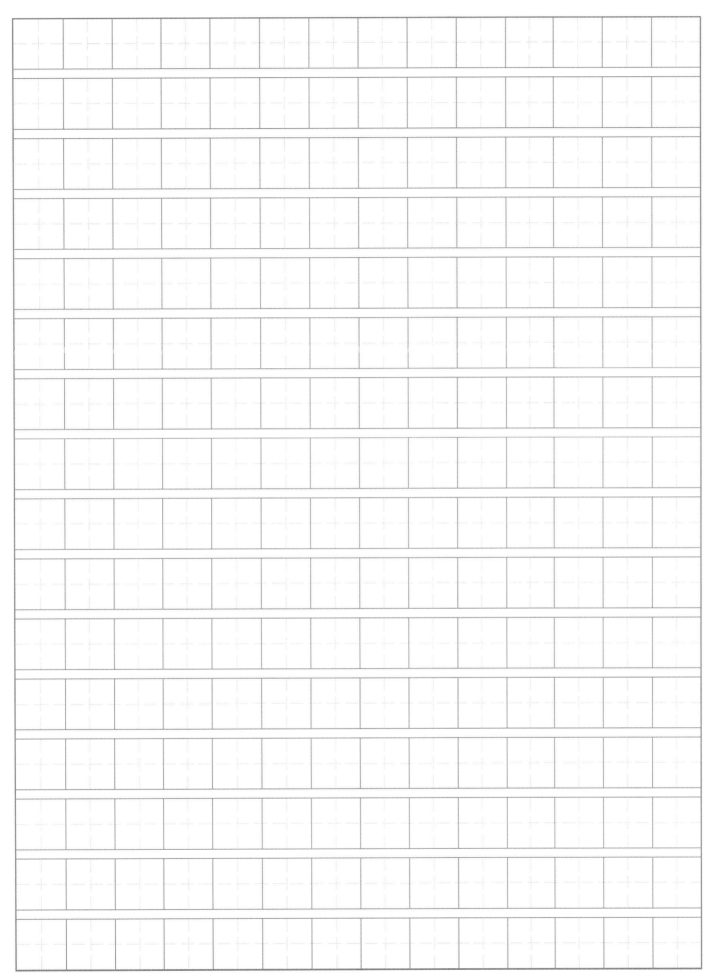

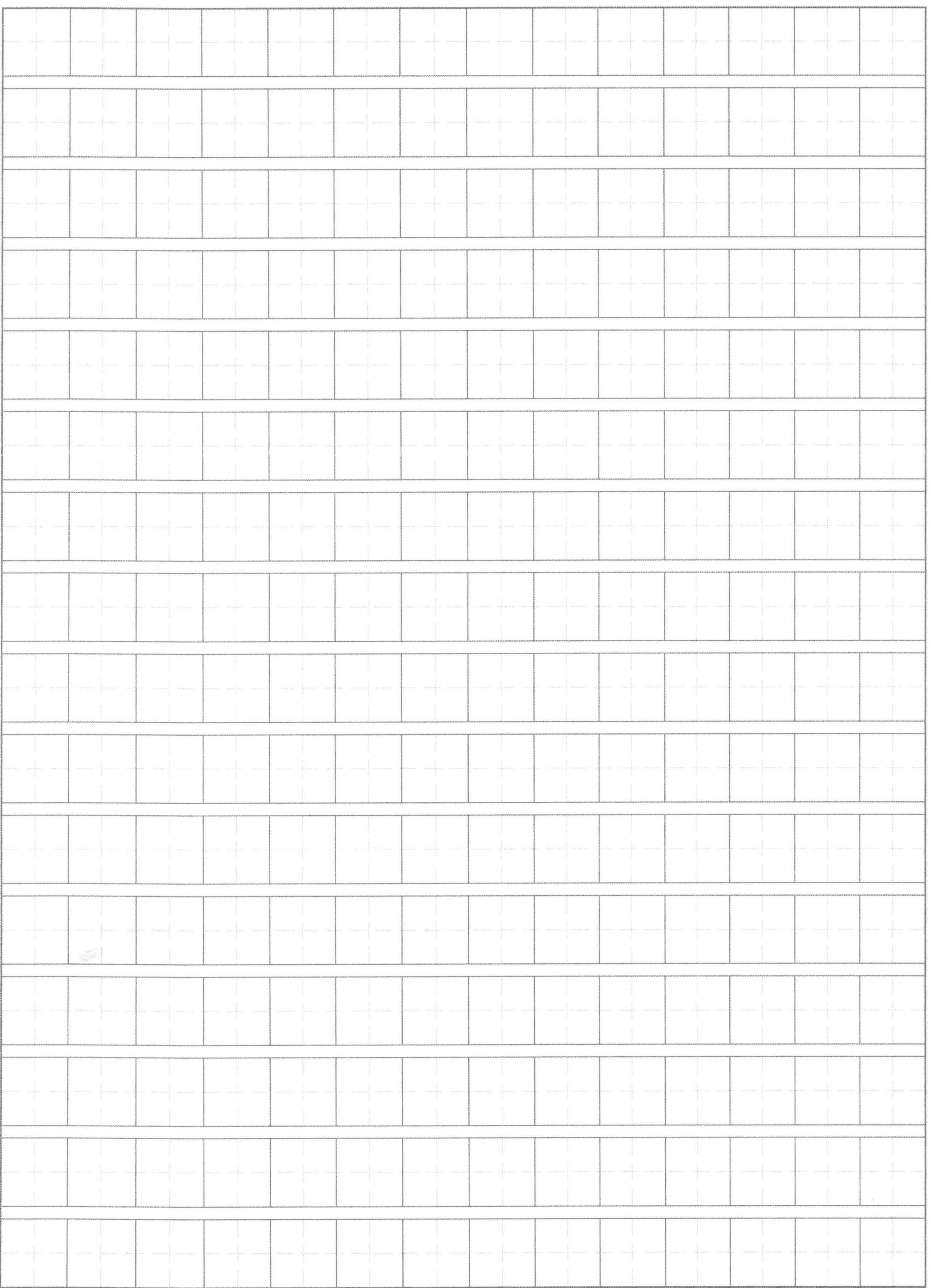

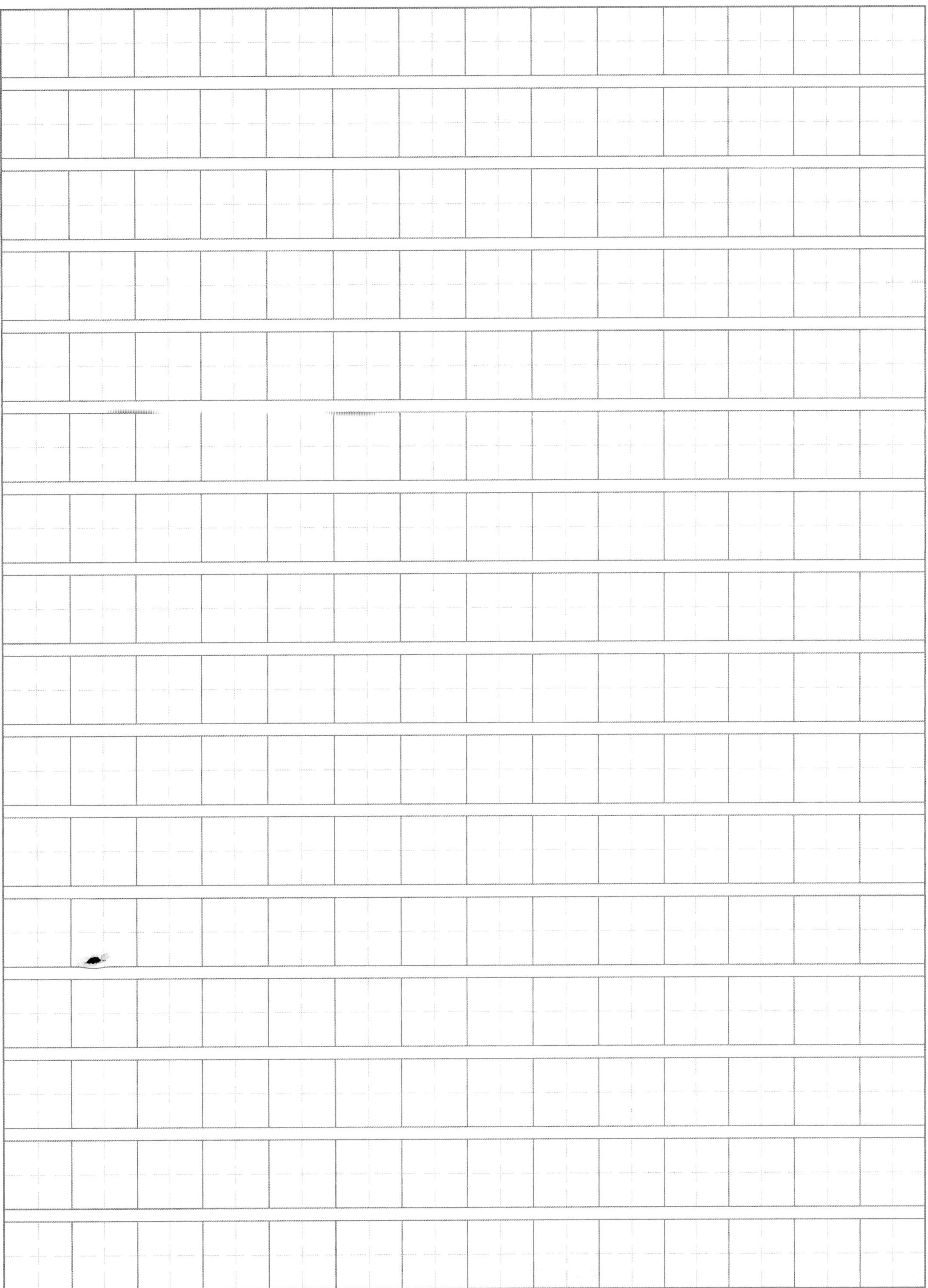

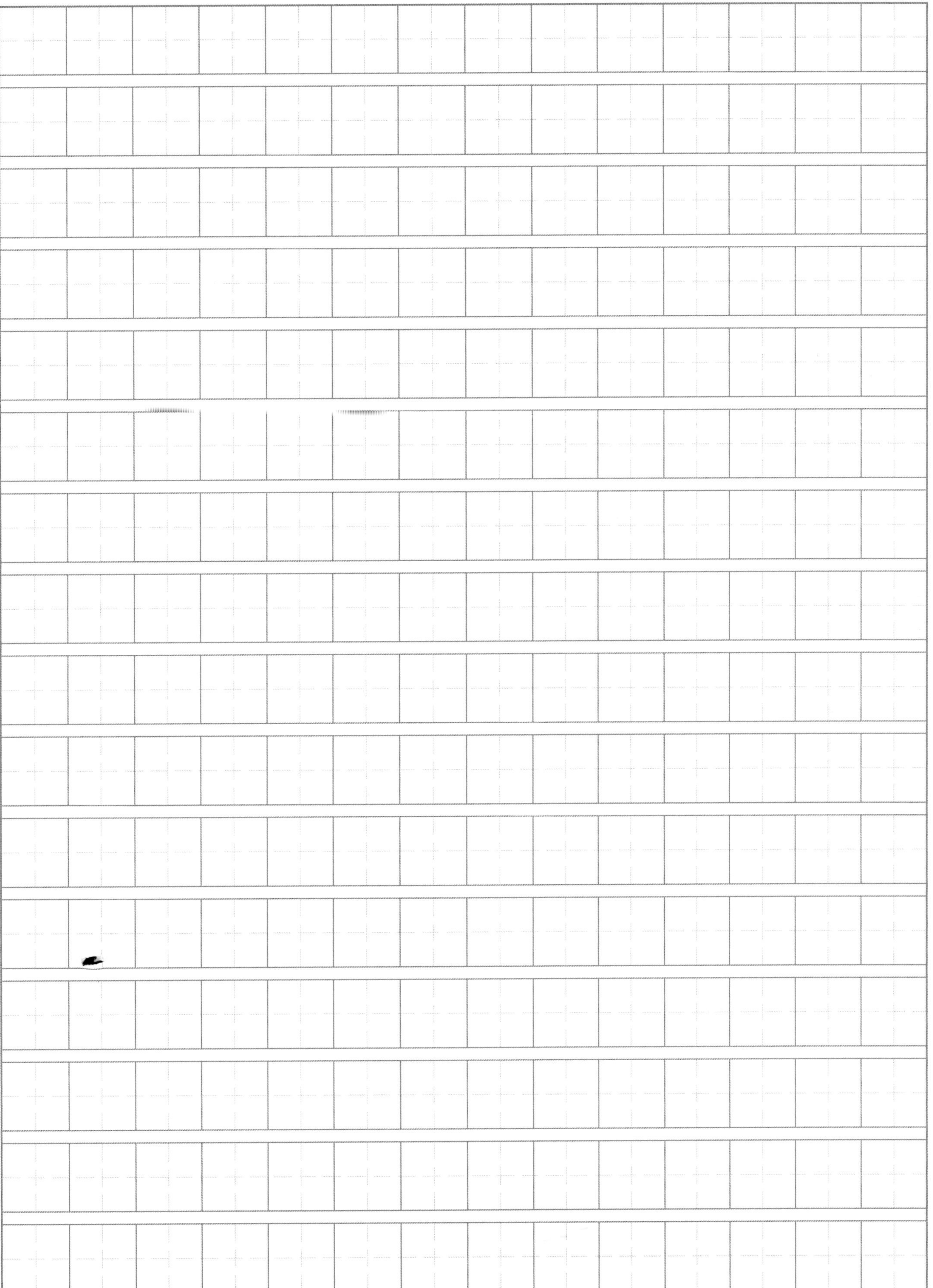

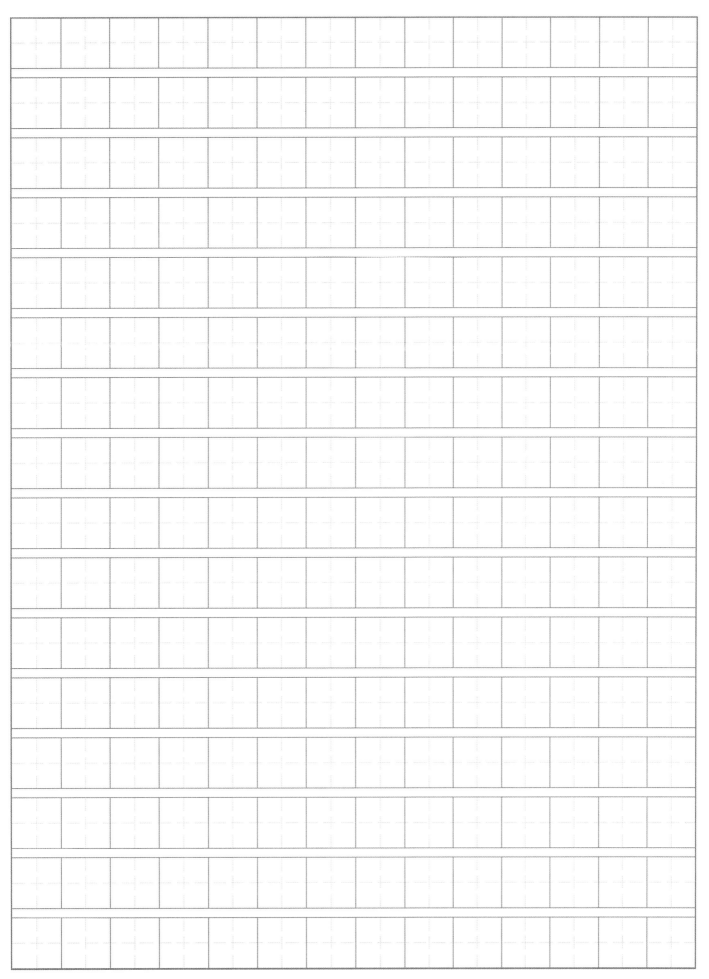

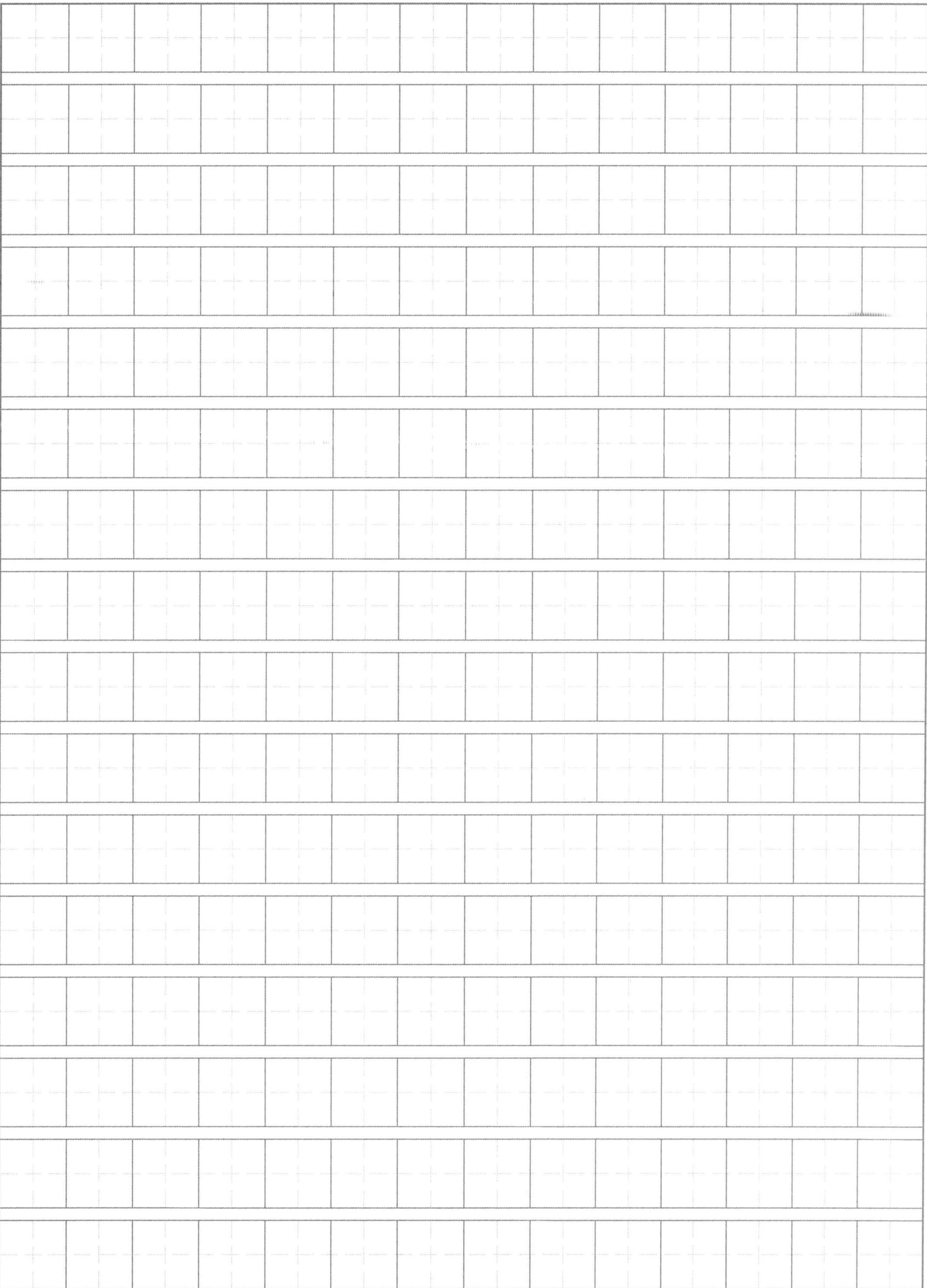

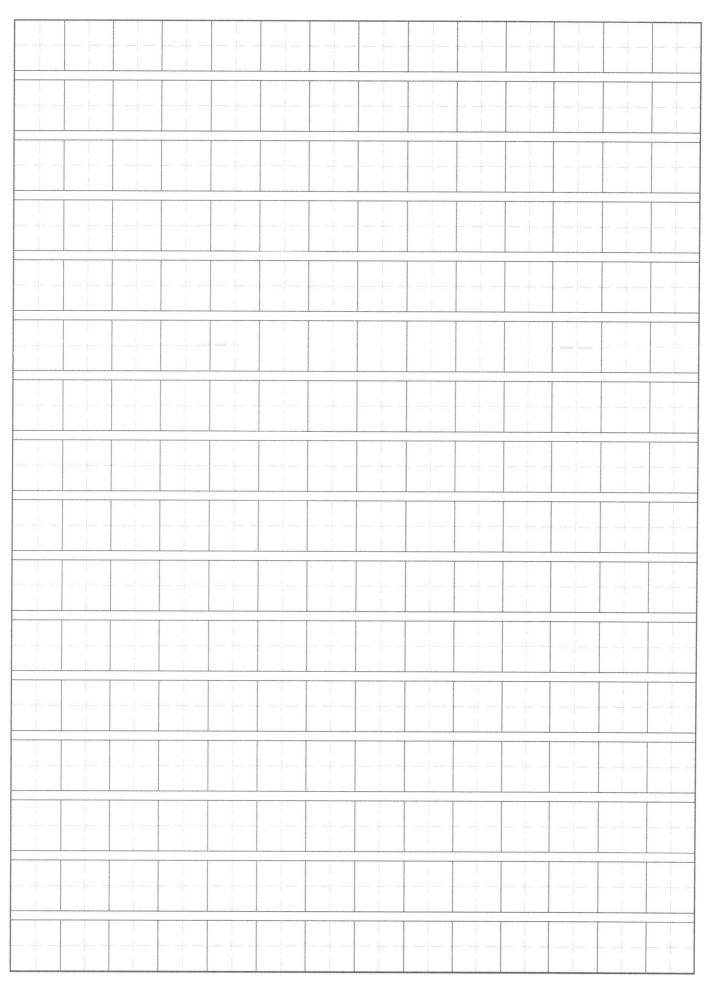

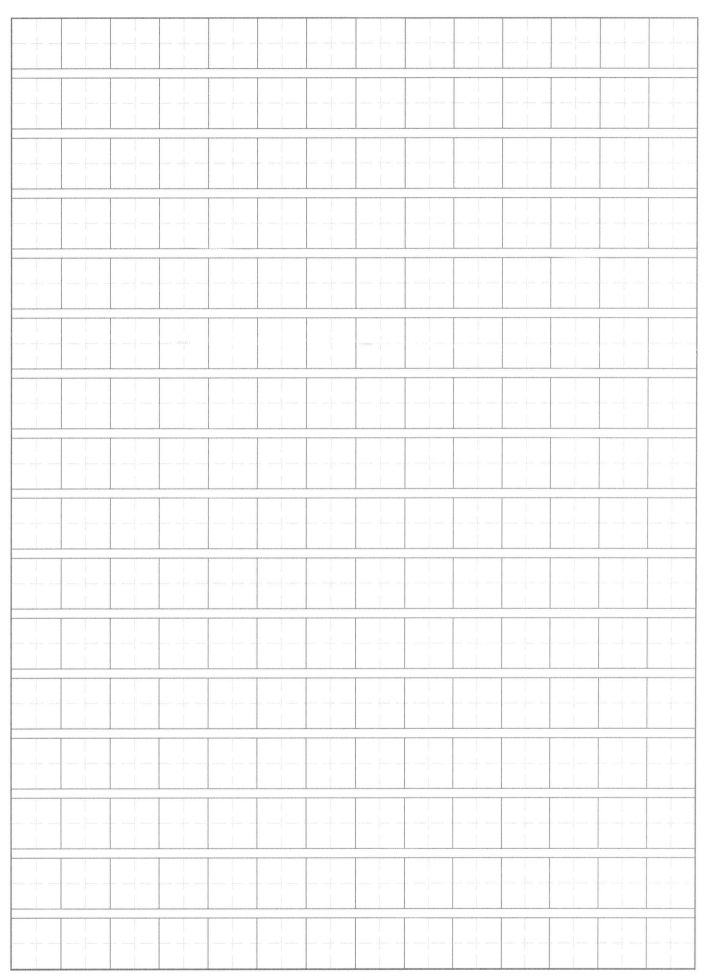

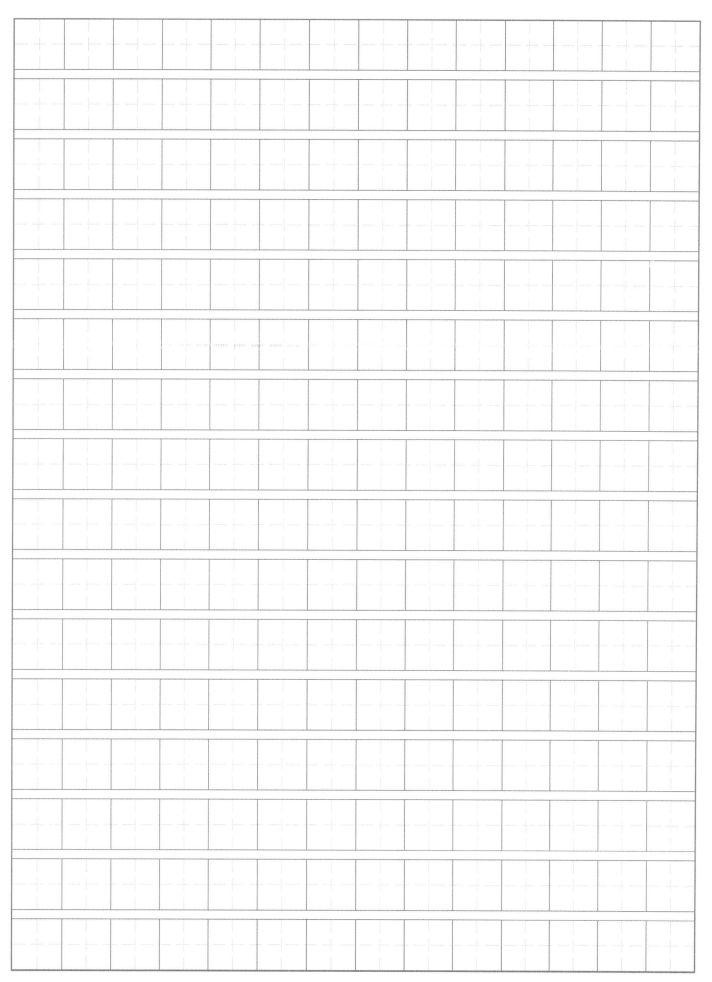

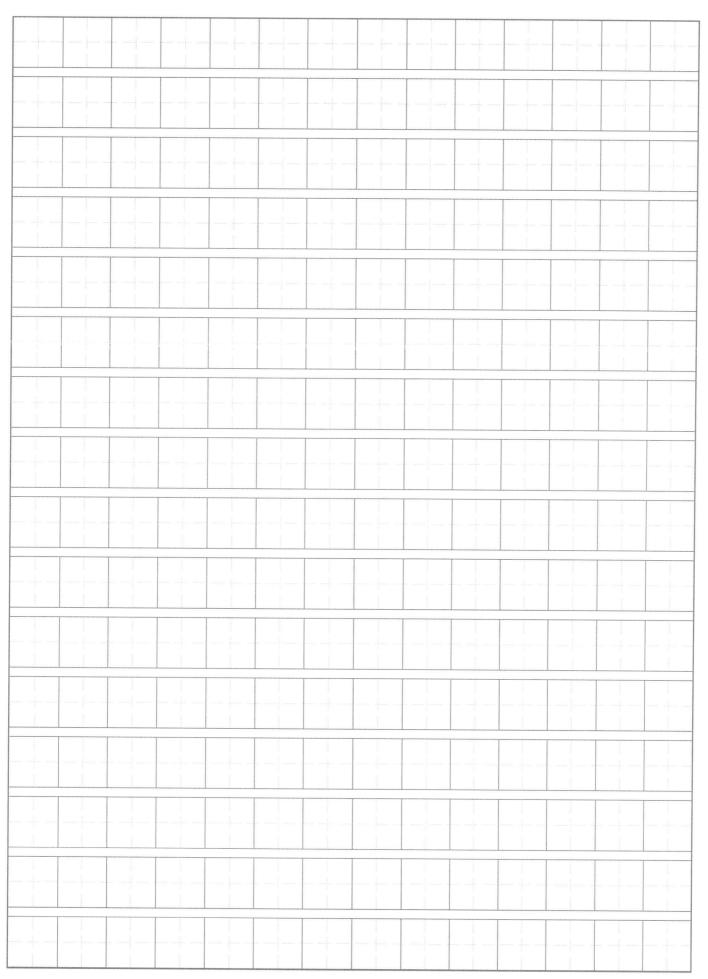

The 46 Basic Hiragana Characters

The chart below shows the 46 basic characters in the hiragana alphabet with their pronunciation. Hiragana is generally used for grammatical endings and words that don't have kanji.

あ a	い i	う u	え e	お o
か ka	き ki	く ku	け ke	こ ko
さ sa	し shi	す su	せ se	そ so
た ta	ち chi	つ tsu	て te	と to
な na	に ni	ぬ nu	ね ne	の no
は ha (wa)	ひ hi	ふ fu	へ he (e)	ほ ho
ま ma	み mi	む mu	め me	も mo
や ya		ゆ yu		よ yo
ら ra	り ri	る ru	れ re	ろ ro
わ wa				を w(o)
ん n				

The 61 Additional Hiragana Characters

Adding two small lines to a hiragana syllable makes the sound hard. *Ka* becomes *ga*, *sa* becomes *za*, etc. Adding a small circle to the syllables starting with *h* makes a *p* sound. In the lower two tables the *i*-column syllable combines with *ya*, *yu* or *yo* to make the sounds *kya*, *kyu*, *kyo*, etc.

が **ga**	ぎ **gi**	ぐ **gu**	げ **ge**	ご **go**
ざ **za**	じ **ji**	ず **zu**	ぜ **ze**	ぞ **zo**
だ **da**	ぢ **ji**	づ **zu**	で **de**	ど **do**
ば **ba**	び **bi**	ぶ **bu**	べ **be**	ぼ **bo**
ぱ **pa**	ぴ **pi**	ぷ **pu**	ぺ **pe**	ぽ **po**

きゃ **kya**	きゅ **kyu**	きょ **kyo**
しゃ **sha**	しゅ **shu**	しょ **sho**
ちゃ **cha**	ちゅ **chu**	ちょ **cho**
にゃ **nya**	にゅ **nyu**	にょ **nyo**
ひゃ **hya**	ひゅ **hyu**	ひょ **hyo**
ぎゃ **gya**	ぎゅ **gyu**	ぎょ **gyo**

じゃ **ja**	じゅ **ju**	じょ **jo**
ぢゃ **ja**	ぢゅ **ju**	ぢょ **jo**
みゃ **mya**	みゅ **myu**	みょ **myo**
りゃ **rya**	りゅ **ryu**	りょ **ryo**
びゃ **bya**	びゅ **byu**	びょ **byo**
ぴゃ **pya**	ぴゅ **pyu**	ぴょ **pyo**

The 46 Basic Katakana Characters

The chart below shows the 46 basic characters in the katakana alphabet with their pronunciation. Katakana is used for writing foreign loan words, for emphasis and for onomatopoeia.

ア a	イ i	ウ u	エ e	オ o
カ ka	キ ki	ク ku	ケ ke	コ ko
サ sa	シ shi	ス su	セ se	ソ so
タ ta	チ chi	ツ tsu	テ te	ト to
ナ na	ニ ni	ヌ nu	ネ ne	ノ no
ハ ha /wa	ヒ hi	フ fu	ヘ h(e)	ホ ho
マ ma	ミ mi	ム mu	メ me	モ mo
ヤ ya		ユ yu		ヨ yo
ラ ra	リ ri	ル ru	レ re	ロ ro
ワ wa				ヲ w(o)
ン n				

The 50 Additional Katakana Characters

Adding two small lines to a katakana syllable makes the sound hard. *Ka* becomes *ga*, *sa* becomes *za*, etc. Adding a small circle to the syllables starting with *h* makes a *p* sound. In the lower two tables the *i*-column syllable combines with *ya*, *yu* or *yo* to make the sounds *kya*, *kyu*, *kyo*, etc.

ガ **ga**	ギ **gi**	グ **gu**	ゲ **ge**	ゴ **go**
ザ **za**	ジ **ji**	ズ **zu**	ゼ **ze**	ゾ **zo**
ダ **da**			デ **de**	ド **do**
バ **ba**	ビ **bi**	ブ **bu**	ベ **be**	ボ **bo**
パ **pa**	ピ **pi**	プ **pu**	ペ **pe**	ポ **po**

キャ **kya**	キュ **kyu**	キョ **kyo**
シャ **sha**	シュ **shu**	ショ **sho**
チャ **cha**	チュ **chu**	チョ **cho**
ニャ **nya**	ニュ **nyu**	ニョ **nyo**
ヒャ **hya**	ヒュ **hyu**	ヒョ **hyo**

ギャ **gya**	ギュ **gyu**	ギョ **gyo**
ジャ **ja**	ジュ **ju**	ジョ **jo**
ミャ **mya**	ミュ **myu**	ミョ **myo**
リャ **rya**	リュ **ryu**	リョ **ryo**

105 Common Kanji Characters

These kanji are often encountered at level N5 of the JLPT test. Beneath each kanji is the English meaning, the *on-yomi* in capitals (the reading generally used in words made up of more than one kanji character), and the *kun-yomi* in bold (the reading generally used for words with one kanji).

一 one ICHI **hito-**	二 two NI **futa-**	三 three SAN **mi-**	四 four SHI **yo-**	五 five GO **itsu-**	六 six ROKU **mu-**	七 seven SHICHI **nana-**
八 eight HACHI **ya-**	九 nine KYŪ **kokono-**	十 ten JŪ **tō**	百 100 HYAKU *no kun reading*	千 1,000 SEN **chi**	万 10,000 MAN/BAN *no kun reading*	円 yen/circle EN **maru-**
日 sun/day NICHI/JITSU **hi/ka**	月 moon/month TSUKI **gatsu/getsu**	火 fire HI/HO **ka**	水 water SUI **mizu**	木 wood/tree MOKU **ki**	金 gold KIN **kane**	土 earth DO/TO **tsuchi**
週 week SHŪ *no kun reading*	年 year NEN **toshi**	時 time JI **toki**	間 between KAN/KEN **aida/ma**	分 minute BUN/FUN **wa-**	午 noon GO **uma-**	前 before ZEN **mae**
後 after GO **ushi-**	今 now KON/KIN **ima**	先 ahead SEN **saki**	半 half HAN **naka-**	毎 every MAI **goto**	何 what KA **nani/nan**	人 person JIN/NIN **hito**
女 woman JO **onna**	男 man DAN **otoko**	子 child SHI/SU **ko**	母 mother BO **haha**	父 father FU **chichi**	友 friend YŪ **tomo**	本 book HON **moto**
川 river SEN **kawa**	山 mountain SAN **yama**	空 sky KŪ **sora**	天 heaven TEN **ama-**	気 spirit KI/KE **iki**	生 life SEI/SHŌ **i-/u-**	雨 rain U **ame**

電 electricity DEN *no kun reading*	車 car SHA **kuruma**	魚 fish GYO **uo/sakana**	語 word GO **kata-**	口 mouth KŌ/KU **kuchi**	目 eye MOKU **me**	耳 ear JI **mimi**
手 hand SHU **te**	足 leg/foot SOKU **ashi**	名 name MEI **na**	店 shop TEN **mise**	駅 station EKI *no kun reading*	道 road DŌ **michi**	社 company SHA **yashiro**
国 country KOKU **kuni**	学 study GAKU **mana-**	校 school KO/KYO *no kun reading*	外 outside GAI **soto**	上 above JŌ/SHŌ **ue**	下 below GE/KA **shita**	中 middle CHŪ **naka**
右 right U/YŪ **migi**	左 left SA **hidari**	北 north HOKU **kita**	南 south NAN **minami**	西 west SEI/SAI **nishi**	東 east TŌ **higashi**	聞 hear/ask BUN/MON **ki(ku)**
見 see KEN **mi(ru)**	読 read DOKU **yo(mu)**	書 write SHO **ka(ku)**	話 speak WA **hana(su)**	言 say GEN **i(u)**	買 buy BAI **ka(u)**	行 go KŌ **i(ku)**
来 come RAI **ku(ru)**	入 go in NYŪ **i(ru)**	出 go out SHUTSU **de(ru)**	休 rest/day off KYŪ **yasu(mu)**	飲 drink IN **no(mu)**	食 eat SHOKU **tabe(ru)**	立 stand RITSU **ta(tsu)**
会 meet KAI **a(u)**	大 big DAI/TAI **ō-**	小 small SHŌ **chī-/ko-**	少 few/little SHŌ **suku(nai)/suko(shi)**	多 many TA **ō-**	安 low/cheap AN **yasu-**	高 high/expensive KŌ **taka-**
古 old KO **furu-**	新 new SHIN **atara-/ara-**	世 world SEISE **yo**	思 think SHI **omo-**	好 like KŌ **kono-/su-**	英 England EI **hanabusa**	引 pull IN **hi-**

100 Common Kanji Vocabulary Words

These vocabulary words are ones that commonly appear in the JLPT N5 test. They include compounds that use the kanji introduced on pages 123–124 as well as common verbs and adjectives that use kanji. Each vocabulary word is presented in three columns, with its kanji reading, its kana reading and its English translation.

1	一人	ひとり	one person
2	二人	ふたり	two people
3	三人	さんにん	three people
4	四月	しがつ	April
5	五月	ごがつ	May
6	六月	ろくがつ	June
7	七日	なのか	7th (date)
8	八日	ようか	8th (date)
9	九日	ここのか	9th (date)
10	十日	とうか	10th (date)
11	千円	せんえん	1,000 yen
12	百万円	ひゃくまんえん	1 million yen
13	万年筆	まんねんひつ	fountain pen
14	日曜日	にちようび	Sunday
15	月曜日	げつようび	Monday
16	火曜日	かようび	Tuesday
17	水曜日	すいようび	Wednesday
18	木曜日	もくようび	Thursday
19	金曜日	きんようび	Friday
20	土曜日	どようび	Saturday
21	毎日	まいにち	every day
22	今日	きょう	today
23	明日	あした	tomorrow
24	昨日	きのう	yesterday
25	何月	なんがつ	what day?
26	今週	こんしゅう	this week
27	来月	らいげつ	next month
28	先月	せんげつ	last month
29	時間	じかん	time
30	十分	じゅっぷん	10 minutes
31	午前	ごぜん	a.m.
32	午後	ごご	p.m.
33	日中	にっちゅう	during the day
34	上着	うわぎ	overcoat, jacket
35	靴下	くつした	socks
36	名前	なまえ	name
37	外国人	がいこくじん	foreigner
38	外国語	がいこくご	foreign language
39	日本語	にほんご	Japanese language
40	英語	えいご	English language
41	女の子	おんなのこ	girl
42	男の子	おとこのこ	boy
43	子供	こども	child
44	花火	はなび	fireworks
45	生徒	せいと	student
46	天気	てんき	weather
47	電気	でんき	electricity
48	元気	げんき	well, fine, healthy
49	手紙	てがみ	letter
50	喫茶店	きっさてん	coffee shop

51	駅前	えきまえ	in front of the station
52	道具	どうぐ	tool
53	会社	かいしゃ	company
54	社長	しゃちょう	company president
55	大学	だいがく	university
56	学校	がっこう	school
57	東京	とうきょう	Tokyo
58	見る	みる	to look; see
59	見せる	みせる	to show
60	聞く	きく	to ask; listen
61	新聞	しんぶん	newspaper
62	書く	かく	to write
63	辞書	じしょ	dictionary
64	読む	よむ	to read
65	言う	いう	to say
66	話す	はなす	to speak
67	電話	でんわ	telephone
68	行く	いく	to go
69	銀行	ぎんこう	bank
70	来る	くる	to come
71	出かける	でかける	to go out
72	出口	でぐち	exit
73	入る	はいる	to go in
74	入口	いりぐち	entrance
75	食べる	たべる	to eat
76	食べ物	たべもの	food
77	飲む	のむ	to drink
78	飲み物	のみもの	drink(s)
79	買う	かう	to buy
80	買い物	かいもの	shopping
81	休む	やすむ	to rest; go on holiday
82	立つ	たつ	to stand
83	大きい	おおきい	big
84	大変	たいへん	dreadful, awful
85	小さい	ちいさい	small
86	高い	たかい	high; expensive
87	安い	やすい	low; cheap
88	多い	おおい	many
89	多分	たぶん	perhaps
90	少ない	すくない	few
91	少し	すこし	a little
92	古い	ふるい	old
93	新しい	あたらしい	new
94	長い	ながい	long
95	部長	ぶちょう	office manager
96	短い	みじかい	short
97	黒い	くろい	black (adj.)
98	白い	しろい	white (adj.)
99	面白い	おもしろい	interesting
100	円い	まるい	round

Plain Verb Forms in Japanese

There are 4 groups of Japanese verbs: *-ru* verbs, *-u* verbs, irregular verbs and special polite verbs, each with a root and a stem. The root is the unchanged core of a verb. The stem is the part of the verb before *-masu*. For *-ru* verbs, the root and stem are the same, ending either in /e/ or /i/. The root of *-u* verbs ends in one of 9 consonants (*b, k, g, m, n, r, t, s, w*), and the stem is the root plus /i/ added at the end. Past Affirmative forms vary according to the consonant. The sound /w/ drops before a vowel, except /a/. Thus /kawu/ becomes /kau/.

	Affirmative			Negative		
	Non-Past	Past	Te Form	Non-Past	Past	Te Form
ru verbs	*Verb* + ru	*Verb* + ta	*Verb* + te	*Verb* + nai	*Verb* + nakatta	*Verb* + nakute
u verbs	waka**ru**	wakatta	wakatte	wakaranai	wakaranakatta	wakaranakute
	ma**tsu**	matta	matte	matanai	matanakatta	matanakute
The largest	ka**(w)**u	katta	katte	kawanai	kawanakatta	kawanakute
group	aso**b**u	asonda	asonde	asobanai	asobanakatta	asobanakute
	no**m**u	nonda	nonde	nomanai	nomanakatta	nomanakute
	shi**n**u	shinda	shinde	shinanai	shinanakatta	shinanakute
	ki**k**u	kiita	kiite	kikanai	kikanakatta	kikanakute
	oyo**g**u	oyoida	oyoide	oyoganai	oyoganakatta	oyoganakute
	hana**s**u	hanashita	hanashite	hanasanai	hanasanakatta	hanasanakute
Four Irregular Verbs	kuru	kita	kite	konai	konakatta	konakute
	suru	shita	shite	shinai	shinakatta	shinakute
	aru	atta	atte	nai	nakatta	nakute
	iku	itta	itte	ikanai	ikanakatta	ikanakute
Five Special Polite Verbs	irassharu	irasshatta	irasshatte	irassharanai	irassharanakatta	irassharanakute
	ossharu	osshatta	osshatte	ossharanai	ossharanakatta	ossharanakute
	nasaru	nasatta	nasatte	nasaranai	nasaranakatta	nasaranakute
	kudasaru	kudasatta	kudasatte	kudasaranai	kudasaranakatta	kudasaranakute
	gozaru	gozatta	gozatte	gozaranai	gozaranakatta	gozaranakute

***ru* verbs:** Non-Past Affirmative:Verb Stem + /ru/
Past Affirmative: Verb Stem + /ta/
Te Form: Verb Stem + /te/
Non-Past Negative: Verb Stem + /nai/
Past Negative: Verb Stem + /nakatta/
Negative Te Form: Verb Stem + /nakute/

***u* verbs:** Non-Past Affirmative: Change the Stem final /i/ to /u/
Past Affirmative: Verb Root + /ta/
Root endings /r/, /t/, or /w/ + /ta/ become /tta/
Root endings /b/, /m/, or /n/ +/ta/ become /nda/
Root ending /k/ + /ta/ becomes /ita/
Root ending /g/ + /ta/ becomes /ida/
Root ending /s/ + /ta/ becomes /shita/
Te Form: Change /ta/ in the Past form to /te/
Non-Past Negative: Verb Root + /anai/
Past Negative: Verb Root + /anakatta/
Negative Te Form: Change /nakatta/ in the past negative form to /nakute/

Published by Tuttle Publishing, an imprint of
Periplus Editions (HK) Ltd.

www.tuttlepublishing.com

Library of Congress Cataloging-in-Publication Data

ISBN 978-4-8053-1612-2

Distributed by

North America, Latin America & Europe
Tuttle Publishing
364 Innovation Drive
North Clarendon, VT 05759-9436 U.S.A.
Tel: 1 (802) 773-8930
Fax: 1 (802) 773-6993
info@tuttlepublishing.com
www.tuttlepublishing.com

Japan
Tuttle Publishing
Yaekari Building 3rd Floor
5-4-12 Osaki
Shinagawa-ku
Tokyo 141-0032
Tel: (81) 3 5437-0171
Fax: (81) 3 5437-0755
sales@tuttle.co.jp
www.tuttle.co.jp

Asia Pacific
Berkeley Books Pte. Ltd.
3 Kallang Sector #04-01
Singapore 349278
Tel: (65) 6741 2178
Fax: (65) 6741 2179
inquiries@periplus.com.sg
www.tuttlepublishing.com

25 24 23 22
11 10 9 8 7 6 5 4 3

Printed in Singapore 2112TP